W9-BSV-850

NATURAL WONDERS OF THE WORLD

GALAPAGOS ISLANDS

Erinn Banting

AV2 BY WEIGL
MEDIA ENHANCED BOOKS
ADDED VALUE · AUDIO VISUAL

www.av2books.com

AV² provides enriched content that supplements and complements this book. Weigl's AV² books strive to create inspired learning and engage young minds in a total learning experience.

Your AV² Media Enhanced books come alive with...

Audio
Listen to sections of the book read aloud.

Video
Watch informative video clips.

Embedded Weblinks
Gain additional information for research.

Try This!
Complete activities and hands-on experiments.

Key Words
Study vocabulary, and complete a matching word activity.

Quizzes
Test your knowledge.

Slideshow
View images and captions, and prepare a presentation.

... and much, much more!

Go to www.av2books.com, and enter this book's unique code.

BOOK CODE

AVP45254

AV² by Weigl brings you media enhanced books that support active learning.

Published by AV² by Weigl
350 5th Avenue, 59th Floor
New York, NY 10118
Website: www.av2books.com

Library of Congress Control Number: 2019938450

ISBN 978-1-7911-0842-7 (hardcover)
ISBN 978-1-7911-0843-4 (softcover)
ISBN 978-1-7911-0844-1 (multi-user eBook)
ISBN 978-1-7911-0845-8 (single-user eBook)

Printed in Guangzhou, China
1 2 3 4 5 6 7 8 9 23 22 21 20 19

052019
311018

Project Coordinator Heather Kissock
Design Ana Maria Vidal and Tammy West

NATURAL
WONDERS
OF THE WORLD

GALAPAGOS ISLANDS

Contents

The Enchanted Isles

The Galapagos Islands, off the coast of South America, are one of the most spectacular **archipelagos** on Earth. They are home to some of the world's most interesting animals. The islands have been the subject of important scientific exploration.

These remote islands were difficult for early explorers to reach. Sailors searching for the islands were blown off their course by strong winds and water **currents**. Some sailors believed the islands had been put under a spell. For this reason, they were nicknamed "the Enchanted Isles."

The Galapagos Islands were first called *Las Encantadas*, which means "The Enchanted" in Spanish.

The **ecosystem** of the Galapagos Islands is unique because of their distance from the South American mainland. These islands also have an unusual climate. The plants and animals living on the islands have had to **adapt** in very interesting ways in order to survive on their island home.

Spotted eagle rays are one of the four kinds of rays that live in the waters of the Galapagos. The other three are manta rays, stingrays, and golden cownose rays.

Galapagos Islands Facts

- The Galapagos Islands are located in the Pacific Ocean, about 600 miles (1,000 kilometers) off the northwest coast of South America.

- The islands cover an area of 23,000 square miles (60,000 sq. km) in the ocean, but only have a land area of 3,086 square miles (7,993 sq. km).

- The Galapagos Islands are owned by Ecuador, a country in northwestern South America.

- The islands are the tops of volcanoes that rise from the seabed.

- The highest point on the islands is a volcano on the island of Isabela that rises to a height of approximately 5,600 feet (1,700 meters).

Mapping the Galapagos Islands

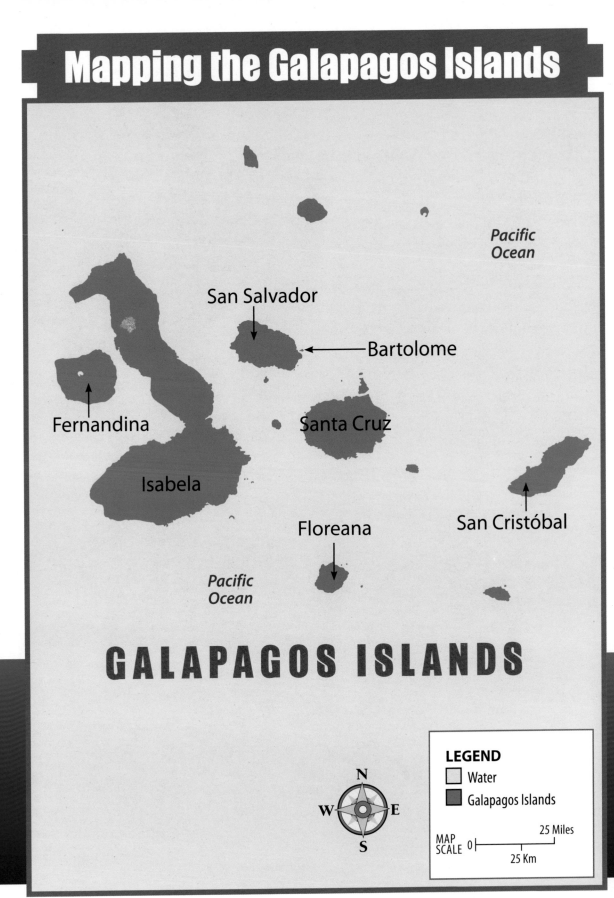

Pacific
Ocean

San Salvador

Bartolome

Fernandina

Santa Cruz

Isabela

San Cristóbal

Floreana

Pacific
Ocean

GALAPAGOS ISLANDS

N

W   E

S

LEGEND

Water

Galapagos Islands

MAP
SCALE   0

25 Miles

25 Km

Where in the World?

The Galapagos Islands are located far off the coast of Ecuador. They are surrounded by the waters of the Pacific Ocean, the largest body of water in the world. The **equator** passes through the northern part of the island chain.

The Galapagos chain consists of a main island called Isabela, 18 other large islands, many smaller islands, and rocks that rise above the water's surface. Beneath the surface of the ocean, many of the islands are connected. They have been formed over millions of years by continuously erupting volcanoes.

Praying Monk is a rock formation on the lava coast of San Salvador Island. This landscape has cliffs and rocks where hundreds of marine birds can come to rest.

One of the most photographed landmarks in the Galapagos is Pinnacle Rock on Bartolome Island. It is the remains of an eroded volcano.

Puzzler

The Galapagos Islands are located in the Pacific Ocean, one of the world's major oceans. **Using an atlas or online source, review the map below and name the world's major island chains. The islands are listed in the box below.**

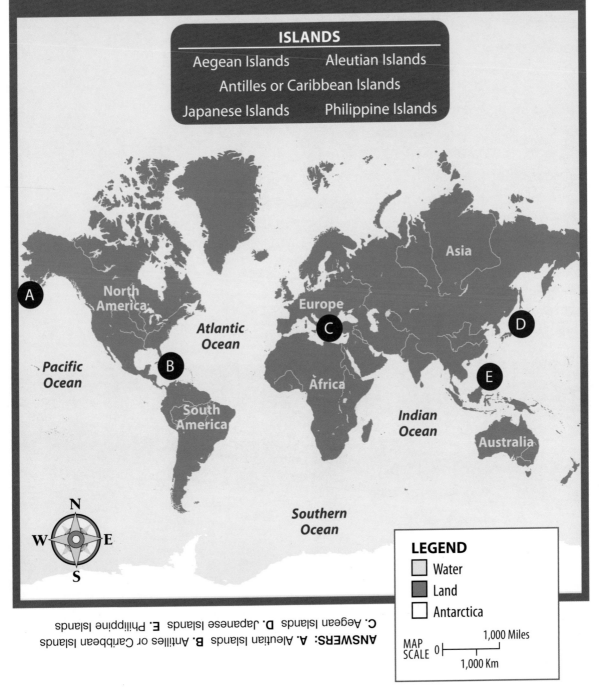

ISLANDS

Aegean Islands   Aleutian Islands

Antilles or Caribbean Islands

Japanese Islands   Philippine Islands

LEGEND
- ☐ Water
- ◼ Land
- ☐ Antarctica

MAP SCALE

0 — 1,000 Miles
0 — 1,000 Km

ANSWERS: A. Aleutian Islands **B.** Antilles or Caribbean Islands **C.** Aegean Islands **D.** Japanese Islands **E.** Philippine Islands

A Trip Back in Time

Hundreds of millions of years ago, Earth's continents were part of a large landmass called Pangaea. Nearly 250 million years ago, this landmass began to split apart. Eventually, two smaller landmasses, the continents of North and South America, slowly drifted to the place where they are today.

The Galapagos Islands were formed much later, between 5 and 9 million years ago. They are the result of volcanic activity below the seabed of the Pacific Ocean that produced giant volcanoes. Over time, **lava** from the volcanoes hardened in layers, creating the landforms above the water that are islands today. Some of these volcanoes are still active and have erupted quite recently. Two of the largest islands in the archipelago, Isabela and Fernandina, experience frequent volcanic eruptions.

The name Pangaea comes from a Greek word meaning "all the Earth."

The Sierra Negra volcano is one of the most active in the Galapagos. It erupted most recently in 2018.

How an Island Forms

Many factors play a part in the way an island is formed. Earth is made up of a crust, a mantle, and a core. The top layer is the crust, which is made up of solid, moving plates. The crust floats on the mantle, a partly **molten** layer. In the crust are chambers of **magma**.

As Earth's crust moves and shifts, magma is pushed up through the cracks or melts a path through the surrounding rocks. Magma erupts as lava at Earth's surface. This pushes up the rock to form a volcano.

The lava is accompanied by gas, ash, and rock fragments. This mixture falls onto the volcano, making it bigger so that it rises above the surface of the ocean to form an island. Over time, the island becomes even larger. As Earth's plates shift, the islands are pushed away from one another, and new islands form. This is how the archipelago in the Galapagos formed.

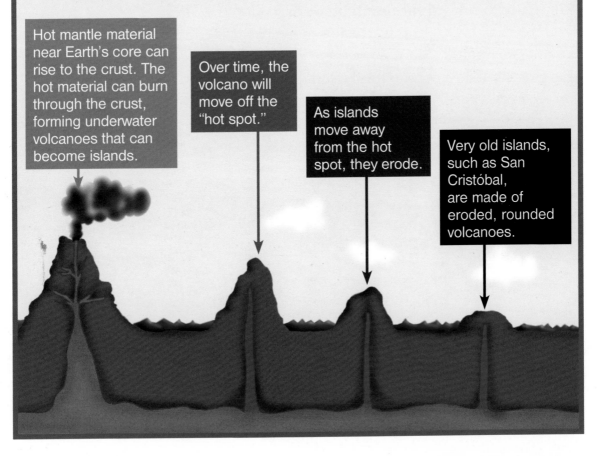

Hot mantle material near Earth's core can rise to the crust. The hot material can burn through the crust, forming underwater volcanoes that can become islands.

Over time, the volcano will move off the "hot spot."

As islands move away from the hot spot, they erode.

Very old islands, such as San Cristóbal, are made of eroded, rounded volcanoes.

The Galapagos Ecosystem

The Galapagos Islands support unique and unusual ecosystems. Their plants and animals have developed separately from related **species** on the distant South American mainland. The Galapagos species have had to adapt to a different climate and different habitats from mainland species. These differences have resulted in the **evolution** of some plants and animals found nowhere else on Earth.

The blue-footed booby's name comes from the Spanish word *bobo*. This means "foolish" or "clown." The blue-footed booby is, like other seabirds, clumsy on land.

On the Galapagos Islands, some species of animals behave differently to related species in other parts of the world. Examples of this are the 13 species of small birds called Galapagos finches. All of them have evolved unique beaks that are shaped to eat the food available on the islands. Some species eat seeds, some eat fruit, and others eat insects. One species called the vampire finch has evolved to feed off the blood and flesh of other birds.

Brightly colored Sally Lightfoot crabs are an important part of the ecosystem. They keep the shore clean of any natural waste and eat ticks off of marine iguanas.

Curious Climate

The Galapagos Islands are located on the equator. In most cases, areas on the equator are very warm and humid. The farther a place is from the equator, the colder its climate tends to be. The frozen North Pole and continent of Antarctica are the farthest places from the equator and are frozen for most of the year.

The climate is cooler in the Galapagos Islands than on any other place on the equator. This is because the islands lie in the path of a cold sea current, called the Humboldt Current. The cold water rises to the surface, bringing tiny plants and animals with it. These creatures provide food for many sea animals.

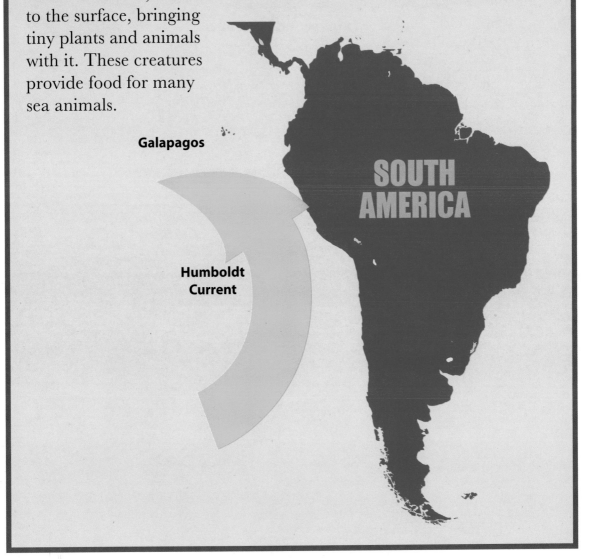

Galapagos

SOUTH AMERICA

Humboldt Current

Life on the Galapagos

Some of the most interesting creatures in the world live on the Galapagos Islands. Flamingos and herons gracefully wade through the coastal waters looking for food. Crabs dart in and out of the waves, looking for shelter and food on sandy beaches or rocky coasts. On the shores, sea lions bask in the sun. Fur seals, which look very similar to sea lions but are much smaller, play in the waves looking for food. They find shelter on the islands' rocky cliffs and shores.

A wide range of plants and flowers grow on the Galapagos Islands. Along the coast, mangrove trees grow because they are able to filter salt water through their roots. Some inland areas are very dry. Plants such as cacti thrive in these conditions. On higher land, a mist from the sea allows flowering plants and tall trees covered with mosses and ferns to flourish.

Red mangroves are found on the island of Isabela. Three other types of mangroves that live in the Galapagos are black, white, and button.

The Galapagos flamingo uses its beak to separate mud and silt from its food. Flamingos can only eat with their heads turned upside down.

The Galapagos Tortoises

The Galapagos Islands are known for, and named after, the 11 species of tortoise that live there. The Spanish word for "tortoise" is *Galapagos*. Each species has unique features.

Tortoises that live in dry, rocky areas have developed shells that curve upward at the neck. This allows them to stretch their long necks upward to eat the tall cacti. Tortoises on wetter islands with more plants at ground level have shorter necks and flatter shells because they can find food close to the ground.

From the 1700s to the mid-1900s, tortoises were hunted for their shells and meat. Sailors often brought cattle, pigs, and goats to the islands. These animals bred and competed with the tortoises for food. Today, the tortoises are protected. It is illegal to hunt them. Some have also been moved to zoos or protected areas so they can breed in safety.

Galapagos tortoises can live to be more than 100 years old in the wild.

Early Explorers

In 1535, the first Europeans landed on the Galapagos Islands. They had been blown off course by the strong Pacific currents. Finding no inhabitants or fresh water, the sailors left the island.

Later, explorers used the islands as a stop for food or supplies on their way to other parts of South America. Pirates also used the islands to hide the jewels, money, and goods they robbed from other ships and from Spanish settlements in Central and South America. Later, hunters and merchants came to the islands to hunt the giant tortoises.

Although they are now empty, pirate caves can still be seen on some of the islands.

No one tried to settle the islands until 1807 when Patrick Watkins, an explorer from Ireland, settled on the island of Floreana. He lived there until 1809, capturing sailors who stopped for supplies and forcing them to work as slaves. Other settlers arrived from the United States and Europe, but it was not until 1832 that the archipelago was officially claimed by Ecuador.

In the early 1900s, only a few hundred people were living on the Galapagos Islands.

Biography

Charles Darwin (1809–1882)

Charles Darwin was a scientific explorer, and his work on the islands is among the most important in the history of science. In 1831, Darwin joined the crew of the HMS *Beagle* to explore the South American coast and the islands in the Pacific Ocean. In 1835, he and the crew traveled to the Galapagos Islands, where he explored the unique **geology**, plants, and animal life on the islands. Darwin observed that many species were different from island to island. He realized that the animals had to adapt to survive where they were. Before Darwin, many people believed that species did not change. In 1859, Darwin wrote a book about his observations and theories called *On the Origin of Species*.

On his visit to the Galapagos Islands, Charles Darwin found that some finches were different from island to island. This showed him how plants and animals change over time.

Facts of Life

- Born: February 12, 1809
- Hometown: Shrewsbury, Shropshire, England
- Occupation: Scientist, explorer
- Died: April 19, 1882

The Big Picture

There are islands surrounding each of Earth's continents. They can be found in both hot and cold climates. Islands support a wide variety of plant and animal life.

LEGEND

- ☐ Water
- ■ Land
- ☐ Antarctica
- ◎ Islands

MAP SCALE

0 — 2,000 Miles
0 — 2,000 Km

North America

South America

Atlantic Ocean

Pacific Ocean

Thousand Islands
Canada

Antilles
Caribbean Sea

Galapagos Islands
Pacific Ocean

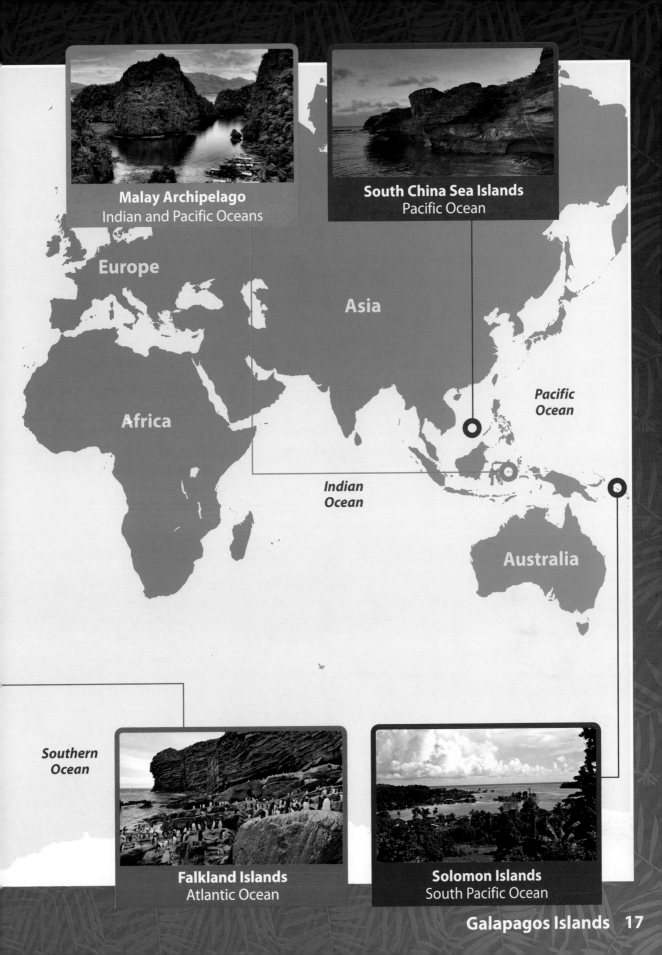

Malay Archipelago
Indian and Pacific Oceans

South China Sea Islands
Pacific Ocean

Europe

Asia

Pacific
Ocean

Africa

Indian
Ocean

Australia

Southern
Ocean

Falkland Islands
Atlantic Ocean

Solomon Islands
South Pacific Ocean

Living on the Galapagos

Though the Galapagos Islands have been home to a wide variety of plant and animal life, there is no evidence to suggest early humans called the islands home. When the Galapagos Islands were discovered in 1535, there were no people living there. Scientists believe this was because the islands were so remote from the South American mainland and because there was not enough fresh water to help people survive and grow crops.

Puerto Baquerizo Moreno is the capital of the Galapagos Province. Fishing is the main activity of the locals, but the tourism industry is increasing.

Today, only four of the islands are inhabited. They are Santa Cruz, Isabela, San Cristóbal, and Floreana. About 30,000 people call the islands home. Most of these people live in the city of Puerto Ayora on Santa Cruz. Many work in the tourism industry, which is the largest industry in the Galapagos.

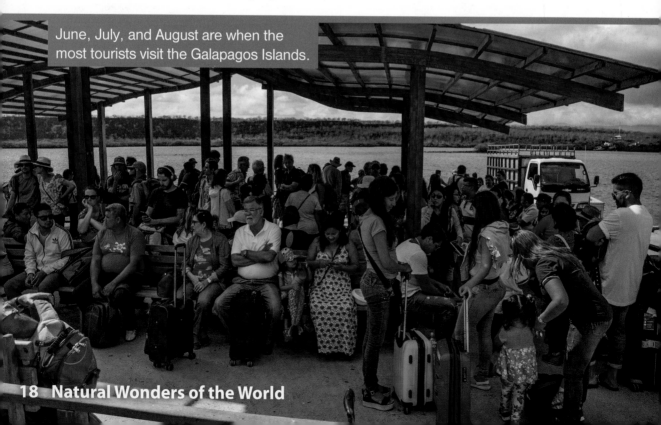

June, July, and August are when the most tourists visit the Galapagos Islands.

Protecting Local Species

The Charles Darwin Research Station is located on the island of Santa Cruz. The station protects the delicate and unique ecosystems of the islands. One of its projects is to save the marine and land tortoises of the Galapagos. The station also works to control species of animals that were introduced to the islands by European explorers. These animals threaten native plant and animal species. There are an estimated 1,700 invasive species in the Galapagos Islands.

The Charles Darwin Research Station also educates young people about the environment and the importance of Earth's ecosystems. Students learn what they can do to help protect our planet. They and other visitors can see an exhibition hall with natural history displays and a garden with native plants.

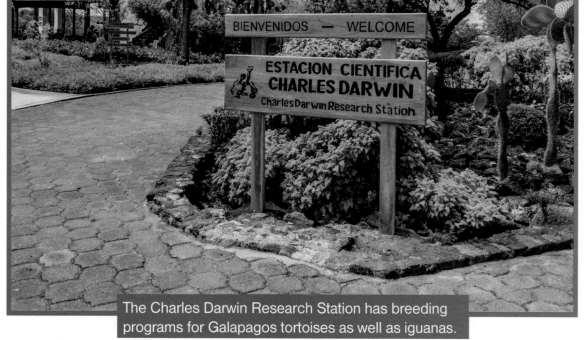

The Charles Darwin Research Station has breeding programs for Galapagos tortoises as well as iguanas.

Timeline

5–9 million years ago
Volcanoes rise from the Pacific Ocean, and the Galapagos Islands form.

1807
Irish explorer Patrick Watkins settles on the island of Floreana.

10 million years ago	1400	1500	1600	1700	1800

1400s
Incas from South America may have been the first people to voyage to the Galapagos Islands.

1535
The Galapagos Islands are discovered by Spanish Bishop Fray Tomás de Berlanga.

1773
English explorer James Cook lands on the Galapagos Islands. One of his crew members, William Dampier, wrote a book about his observations on the wildlife of the islands.

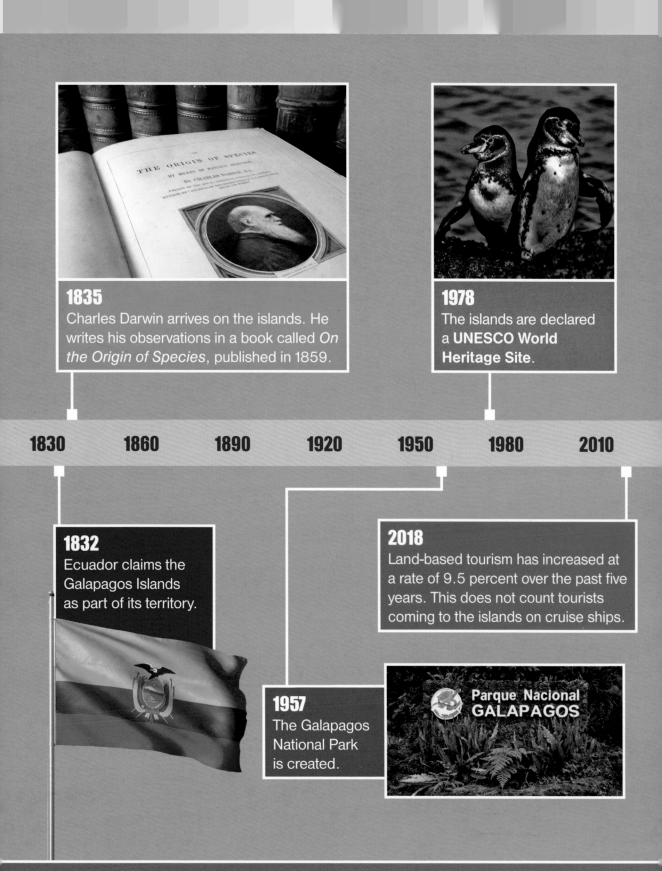

1835
Charles Darwin arrives on the islands. He writes his observations in a book called *On the Origin of Species*, published in 1859.

1978
The islands are declared a **UNESCO World Heritage Site**.

1830   1860   1890   1920   1950   1980   2010

1832
Ecuador claims the Galapagos Islands as part of its territory.

2018
Land-based tourism has increased at a rate of 9.5 percent over the past five years. This does not count tourists coming to the islands on cruise ships.

1957
The Galapagos National Park is created.

Parque Nacional GALAPAGOS

Protecting the Galapagos

The waved albatross, or Galapagos albatross, is the largest bird on the islands. Its main threat is getting caught in hooks meant to catch fish.

Many factors have posed a threat to the delicate Galapagos Islands environment. These include hunting, whaling, and fishing. The arrival of humans and the introduction of foreign plants and animals have also damaged life on the archipelago.

Today, scientists work hard to protect the islands and their creatures. The islands have been protected by the government of Ecuador since 1935. In 1978, the islands were also named a UNESCO World Heritage Site. UNESCO works to protect unique ecosystems and geographical regions, as well as the people, plants, and animals that inhabit them.

Introduced species, such as goats, cats, and dogs, have been hunted and removed in order to protect the food chain. These non-native animals take food away from native species, such as tortoises and finches. The island of San Salvador had more than 80,000 non-native goats, which have now been eradicated. Wild goats and donkeys have also been removed from Isabela Island. The hope is that, with the goats and donkeys gone, native finches and other birds, as well as native plants and trees, will be able to thrive.

The Galapagos fur seal is an endangered species, meaning it is at risk of dying out and no longer being found anywhere on Earth.

Should hunting introduced species on the Galapagos Islands be allowed?

Yes	No
The animals threaten the native species and the balance of the fragile ecosystem.	It is cruel to hunt these animals. They should be trapped and removed from the island instead.
Some of the animals can be used for food and their hides.	Some, such as cats and dogs, cannot be hunted. These animals should be taken into shelters.
If they are not hunted, the introduced species may eliminate the native species.	Scientists can find ways to protect the native species, such as nature reserves.

From 1997 to 2006, people worked to remove all 250,000 goats from the Galapagos Islands.

Natural Attractions

More than 225,000 tourists visit the Galapagos Islands every year. They come to see the curious creatures and breathtaking sights. Many people visit the Charles Darwin Research Station to see giant tortoises close up. Visitors can travel from island to island in search of other unique creatures, such as marine iguanas, penguins, and sea lions.

Scuba divers and snorkelers come to the Galapagos Islands to see unique coral reefs.

People also participate in water sports and explore the wildlife beneath the surface of the ocean. Snorkeling, scuba diving, and sailing are all popular activities along the coasts. Boat tours and cruises give people a different view.

There are also countless interesting rock formations and natural landforms to explore on the Galapagos Islands. On the island of Isabela, people can tour the many volcanoes. Most islands also have curious rock formations created by lava.

Tourists can be just inches (centimeters) away from captive Galapagos tortoises at the Charles Darwin Research Station.

Recipe

Humitas are traditional South American dumplings. They are a popular treat on the Galapagos Islands. With the help of an adult, you can make these delicious corn and cheese dumplings for your family and friends.

You will need:
- 3 cups (750 grams) fresh ground corn
- 3 tbsp (45 g) butter
- 2 tbsp (30 g) grated cheese, any type
- 1/2 tsp (2.5 g) salt
- 1/2 tbsp (7.5 g) flour
- 2 eggs
- 9 corn husks

What to do:
1. Melt the butter in a frying pan.
2. In a mixing bowl, combine the melted butter, ground corn, cheese, salt, flour, and eggs.
3. Stir the mixture together.
4. Wash the corn husks.
5. Place a spoonful of mixture in the center of each husk.
6. Fold the husks over the mixture.
7. Place in a pot, and steam for 45 minutes.

Legends from the Galapagos

Though the Galapagos Islands were officially discovered by Europeans in 1535, legends of the Inca people in South America suggest they may have discovered them earlier. According to one legend, a group of sailors reported seeing an "island of fire," which may have been one of the erupting volcanoes of the Galapagos.

Spewing lava can look much like a burning fire.

Many stories from the Galapagos Islands are about the giant tortoises. One story involves a giant tortoise and a British explorer named James Cook, who lived between 1728 and 1779. According to the story, Cook landed on the islands in 1773 and captured a giant tortoise. To mark his voyage, Cook carved the year on the tortoise's back. To this day, people have reported seeing the tortoise on different islands. No one is sure if it is the tortoise from the legend.

James Cook explored islands throughout the Pacific Ocean. He made maps that later helped other explorers.

Post Office Bay

Post Office Bay, on the island of Floreana, is one of the best-known and most visited places on the Galapagos Islands. The bay is famous because it was the location for the islands' postal service. In 1793, a whale hunter named James Colnett placed a wooden barrel by the bay for people to put their letters in. Many ships stopped in the bay, and when they did, they picked up letters to take back to Europe and dropped off letters for other sailors who were on long voyages.

Today, tourists visit the bay. A wooden barrel still sits on its shores. People can take letters from the barrel, and when they return home, send the letters to the person for whom they were intended. People can also leave their own letters for someone else to send.

Piles of driftwood and artifacts, covered in graffiti and stickers that have been brought by past visitors, surround the barrel on Post Office Bay.

What Have You Learned?

True or False?

Decide whether the following statements are true or false.
If the statement is false, make it true.

1. There are three species of tortoises living on the Galapagos Islands.

2. The Galapagos Islands belong to Brazil.

3. Charles Darwin was a scientist who studied the plants and animals of the Galapagos Islands.

4. The Galapagos Islands are located off the northwest coast of South America.

5. People do not live on the Galapagos Islands.

6. The waved albatross is the largest bird on the Galapagos Islands.

ANSWERS: 1. False. There are 11 species of tortoises living on the islands. **2.** False. The Galapagos Islands belong to Ecuador. **3.** True **4.** True **5.** False. Several of the islands are inhabited. **6.** True

Short Answer

Answer the following questions using information from the book.

1. What is an archipelago?

2. Why do the Galapagos Islands have a cool climate?

3. How many people visit the Galapagos Islands each year?

4. Where is the Charles Darwin Research Station located?

5. What is unique about the wildlife species on the Galapagos Islands?

ANSWERS: 1. A chain of islands **2.** The Humboldt Current flows north from Antarctica to the islands. **3.** More than 225,000 **4.** The island of Santa Cruz **5.** Many do not exist anywhere else in the world.

Multiple Choice

Choose the best answer for the following questions.

1. Where did the Galapagos Islands get their name?

    a. From the French word for tiger
    b. From the Japanese word for bear
    c. From the Spanish word for tortoise
    d. From the Italian word for fish

2. What is the equator?

    a. An imaginary line that divides
       Earth into two parts
    b. Another name for the North Pole
    c. A type of cactus
    d. A water current

3. What animal species has evolved from eating plants to eating flesh and blood on the Galapagos Islands?

    a. The vampire iguana
    b. The vampire finch
    c. The vampire tortoise
    d. The vampire penguin

4. What is the name of the main island?

    a. Isabela
    b. Floreana
    c. Fernandina
    d. Bartolome

ANSWERS: 1. c 2. a 3. b 4. a

Activity

Volcanic Activity

Millions of years ago, volcanoes deep in the Pacific Ocean erupted. The lava cooled, and eventually created the Galapagos Islands. Try this experiment to see how volcanoes erupt and how the "lava" pours up and out.

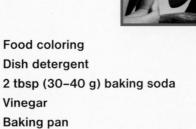

Materials

3 cups (375 g) flour	Food coloring
1 cup (273 g) salt	Dish detergent
1 cup (237 ml) water	2 tbsp (30–40 g) baking soda
2 tbsp (30 ml) vegetable oil	Vinegar
Empty 20-oz (591 ml) drink bottle	Baking pan

Instructions

1. Mix the flour, salt, water, vegetable oil, and a few drops of food coloring in a large bowl until the mixture is smooth.

2. Fill the empty drink bottle almost all the way full with hot tap water. Add a squirt (5–7 drops) of dishwashing detergent and 2 tbsp (30–40 grams) of baking soda. You may wish to add a few drops of food coloring to the bottle. Put the drink bottle in the center of the baking pan.

3. Press the dough around the bottle until it is covered and shaped like a volcano. Do not plug the bottle opening or drop volcano dough in the bottle.

4. Slowly pour some vinegar into the plastic drink bottle and watch your volcano erupt!

5. To repeat the experiment, add more baking soda to the bottle and then pour in more vinegar.

Results

You saw the volcano erupt and the "lava" flow down its sides and into the baking pan. If you repeated this experiment often enough, the lava would begin to build up in the pan, just as lava builds up on the ocean floor and forms islands.

Key Words

adapt: to change based on one's surroundings or requirements

archipelagos: groups, or chains, of islands

currents: moving bodies of water below the ocean surface

ecosystem: a community of organisms and the environment in which they live

equator: the imaginary line that divides Earth into two parts

evolution: the process by which a species changes over time

geology: the study of rocks

lava: melted rock from inside Earth that reaches the surface

magma: melted rock between Earth's crust and core

molten: liquefied by heat

species: a group of plants or animals with the same characteristics

UNESCO World Heritage Site: a place that is of natural or cultural importance to the entire world. UNESCO is an abbreviation for United Nations Educational, Scientific, and Cultural Organization.

Index

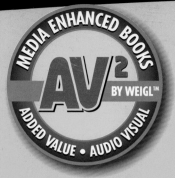

Log on to www.av2books.com

AV² by Weigl brings you media enhanced books that support active learning. Go to www.av2books.com, and enter the special code found on page 2 of this book. You will gain access to enriched and enhanced content that supplements and complements this book. Content includes video, audio, weblinks, quizzes, a slideshow, and activities.

AV² Online Navigation

Book Pages
AV² pages directly correspond to pages in the book.

Key Words
Study vocabulary, and complete a matching word activity.

Quizzes
Test your knowledge.

Slideshow
View images and captions, and prepare a presentation.

Audio
Listen to sections of the book read aloud.

Video
Watch informative video clips.

Embedded Weblinks
Gain additional information for research.

Try This!
Complete activities and hands-on experiments.

AV² was built to bridge the gap between print and digital. We encourage you to tell us what you like and what you want to see in the future.

Sign up to be an AV² Ambassador at www.av2books.com/ambassador.

Due to the dynamic nature of the internet, some of the URLs and activities provided as part of AV² by Weigl may have changed or ceased to exist. AV² by Weigl accepts no responsibility for any such changes. All media enhanced books are regularly monitored to update addresses and sites in a timely manner. Contact AV² by Weigl at 1-866-649-3445 or av2books@weigl.com with any questions, comments, or feedback.